# Fantastic Sports

# Snow-
# BOARDING

## Lesley McKenna

This edition printed in 2000

© Aladdin Books Ltd 1998

*Designed and produced by*
**Aladdin Books Ltd**
28 Percy Street
London W1P 0LD

ISBN 0 7496 3893 1 (paperback)

*First published in Great Britain
in 1998 by*
**Aladdin Books/Watts Books**
96 Leonard Street
London
EC2A 4XD

*Editor*
Sarah Levete

*Design*
David West
Children's Book Design

*Designer*
Flick Killerby

*Illustrators*
Richard Rockwood
Catherine Ward – Simon Girling &
Associates

*Picture Research*
Brooks Krikler Research

This title was previously published in
hardback as The Fantastic Fold-out
Book of Snowboarding

ISBN 0 7496 3100 7 (hardback)

Equipment supplied by Boardwise,
Tamworth and Boardwise, Chiswick

The author, Lesley McKenna, is the
British Ladies Snowboarding
champion.

The consultant, Steve Ensor
(BSA/BASI), is a snowboard instructor
and a representative for the British
Snowboarding Association.

Printed in Belgium

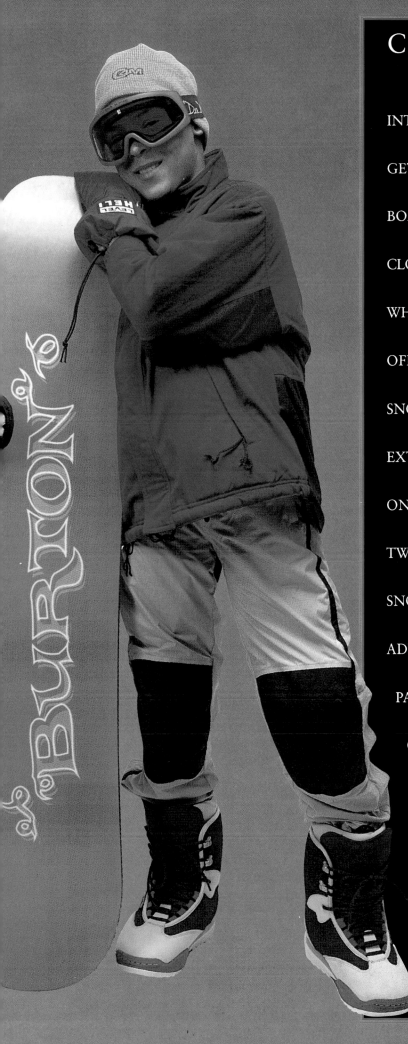

# CONTENTS

# Introduction

Snowboarding is fun, fast and demanding. Whatever your age, whatever your ability, snowboarding has something to offer you. Read on, board up and hit the snow… or the dry ski slope.

Originally invented over twenty years ago by some American surfers, snowboarding is now the fastest-growing winter sport – but you can do it during the summer, too! In snowboarding's early days boarders were not even allowed on the hills of ski resorts, but today many resorts encourage and welcome boarders.

There's a buzz to snowboarding. It's not just a sport, it's a way of life, too, influencing the fashion and music of today. Like other "extreme" sports, such as skateboarding and in-line skating, snowboarding is continually developing, as riders discover new and exciting challenges (*right*).

Snowboarding can be dangerous – you need to be very aware of safety, at all times. Begin with some lessons with a qualified instructor on a dry ski slope, or, if you live near a snowy area, begin on the real thing.

Whether or not you are an experienced rider, this book tells you everything you need to know about snowboarding from putting on your bindings to taking some air, or jumping.

As long as you are fit and healthy, you can enjoy the freedom and challenge of snowboarding. Whatever you do, and whatever your level, stay safe and have fun!

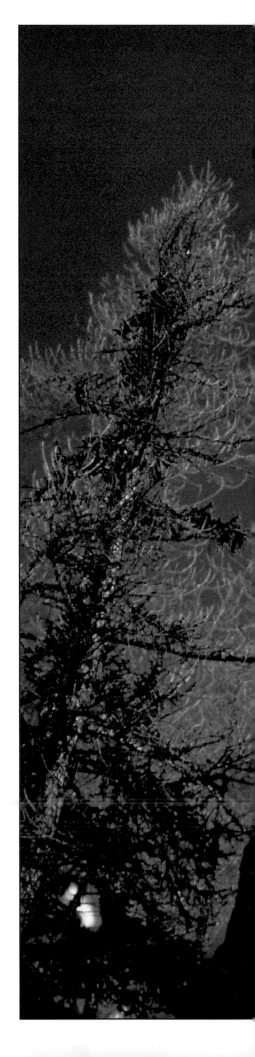

4

# Getting into snowboarding

From free-riding to racing, there are several snowboarding styles – with new ones developing all the time. As a beginner, you need to learn the basic techniques and skills before you start experimenting with different styles.

Snowboarding is about feeling free and doing what you want to do in your own way, safely. Pick up your board, take along your sense of humour, and have a go!

*FREE-RIDING*
*Free-riding gives you the best of every snowboarding style – you are free to choose from all of them! Free-riders make use of all the different types of snow and terrain, from deep powder – light, fluffy snow – to bumps and moguls (see page 24). As a free-rider, you can ride at speed, find a big jump or just glide gently along a field of fresh snow.*

Take your pick!

*In free-style, snowboarders "take air" and "pull tricks" in the park (an area with jumps) and the half-pipe (a channel carved out of the snow, above).*

*Racing (above) is a timed discipline in which riders try to pick the fastest line around "gates" or poles set in the snow.*

6

## FOLLOW THE SNOW... OR THE DENDEX

Many schools run trips to ski resorts where boarders are welcome. This can be a great opportunity to try out snowboarding.

The best places to ride are in the European Alps or the large American or Canadian ski resorts. Other places to ride include Argentina, Austria, Australia, Chile, Greece, Italy, New Zealand, Scotland, South Africa and Turkey!

Dry slopes, made of a material called Dendex, are very popular too, with beginners and experienced riders.

*GETTING RELATED*

*Although its direct relation is the traditional sport of skiing (bottom right), snowboarding is known as an extreme sport – highly skilful but possibly dangerous – so safety is crucial. Other "extreme" sports which appeal particularly to young people are in-line skating, surfing (below left), BMX bike riding (below right), and skateboarding (bottom left). Snowboarding has been described as skateboarding or surfing on snow!*

*Extreme snowboarding (see page 17) involves skill and courage as the rider tackles slopes and drops off the beaten track (above).*

## SNURFING TO SNOWBOARDING

Snowboarding is only about 20 years old. It began when American surfer Sherman Poppen designed a "snurfer", two skis bolted together for surfing on snow, rather than water! Soon, American snurf enthusiast Jake Burton changed the design of his snurfer, and the first basic snowboards began to hit the slopes. These early boards with foot straps were a long way from the high-tech equipment of today. As more and more people took their boards to the snow, the International Snowboard Federation (ISF) was set up as the worldwide governing body for the sport. Today, snowboarding is recognised as an Olympic sport.

## BINDING YOUR BOOTS

Soft boots (*right*) are the most popular. They are usually used with high-back bindings with two straps. These provide good ankle support. Many riders are now using step-in soft boots, which clip onto the board. Hard boots are used for racing.

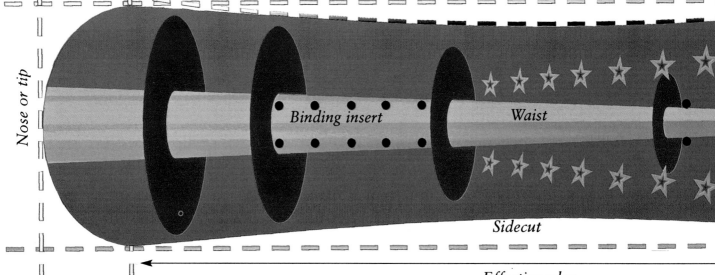

*Contact point*

*Nose or tip*

*Binding insert*

*Waist*

*Sidecut*

*Effective edge*

**View of the board from above**

*Shovel, or curve of the nose*

*Camber*

**View of the board from the side**

## STANCE WIDTH

Once you have decided whether you are goofy or regular (*see page 9*), you can set up your board with your stance width. This is the distance between the centre points of your bindings (*right*). As a guide, your feet should be about shoulder width apart but the best stance width is really the one which feels most comfortable for you. If your stance is too wide, you cannot turn; if it is too narrow, you will not have good balance.

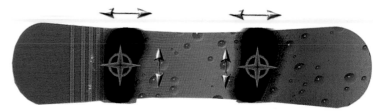

**Binding inserts allow you to adjust the stance width.**

*Once you have found a comfortable width, you need to set the angles (right). Most free-riders and free-stylers ride with between 10° and 30° on the front foot and 3° to 15° on the back foot.*

## BASIC BOARD FACTS

The nose, or tip, and tail of the board curve up, allowing the board to float over the snow. The "effective edges" are the sharp metal edges which are in contact with the snow. The waist of the board gives the sidecut, the curve of the board's edge. A small waist means a quicker turn.

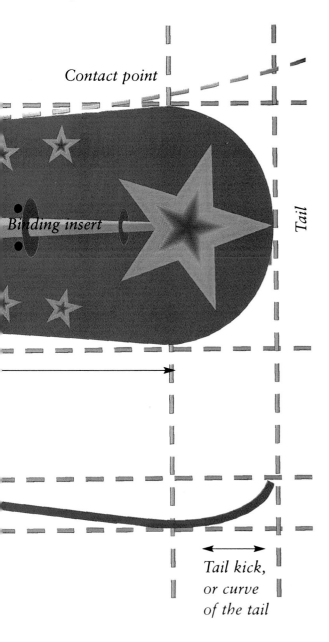

*Contact point*

*Binding insert*

*Tail*

*Tail kick, or curve of the tail*

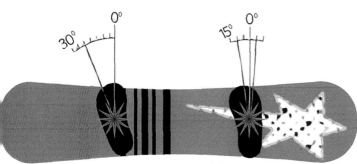

Binding inserts allow you to adjust the stance angle.

# Boarding equipment

There are many different types and makes of boards and boots – but don't panic. As a beginner, start with soft boots with high-back bindings and use a free-ride/free-style board. The bindings, which can be adjusted, secure your boots to the board. With this set-up, you can enjoy all kinds of riding, on all kinds of snow.

If, after a while, you want to specialise in one kind of riding, such as racing, you can then change your equipment.

**REGULAR OR GOOFY?**
If you snowboard with your left foot forwards, or leading, (the one closest to the board's tip or nose) you are regular (*left*); if you snowboard with your right foot forwards, you are goofy (*below*).

To find out if you are regular or goofy, ask a friend to push you gently forwards. Whichever foot you put down to steady yourself is your leading or front foot, and should be the one leading on your board.

**DO YOUR BOOTS FIT?**
Whether you are hiring boots or buying them, take your time. They need to fit well for comfort and skilful riding.

Your boots should feel comfortable, like trainers. You want to be able to wiggle your toes, but you should not be able to lift up your heels.

It is a good idea to take a pair of ski socks to put on when you buy or hire boots.

9

# Clothing for safety and comfort

Snowboarding is about style so it is important to look good as well as to feel comfortable and be safe. There are many makes of snowboard clothing to choose from. If you are going to ride on snow, you need warm, waterproofed clothing. If you are riding on a dry ski slope you will need cooler but harder-wearing materials.

Accessories such as goggles aren't just there to look good – they are there for safety and protection.

### HOW'S YOUR HEAD?
Snowboarding can be dangerous. Always wear a helmet when you are a beginner, and particularly if the snow is icy. Even the most experienced riders wear helmets and most people wear them in the pipe and park (*see pages 26-27*). Not all shops sell snowboarding helmets for young people – an in-line skating helmet (*above*) or a mountain bike helmet will do just as well. Wear a woolly hat for warmth underneath. With goggles (*above*), too, you can look pretty cool.

### SUN SENSE
When you are high up in the mountains, your skin and eyes are exposed to strong sunlight, magnified by the glare from the snow. Sun rays can burn you, even when it is very cold. Apply some lip protection and cover your face with a high factor (20+) sunscreen or sun-block. This will also protect your skin from the wind and cold. Shield your eyes from the sun with a good pair of goggles or sunglasses.

### UNDERNEATH...?
What you wear under your snowboarding clothes is important for comfort and warmth. If it is cold wear many layers of light clothing which trap air to keep you warm but which can also be removed if you get too hot. Natural fibres, such as cotton, stop you from sweating too much.

— *Inner gloves*

— *A fleece sweatshirt is light, warm and hard-wearing – wear it over a thermal vest. It also dries easily if it gets wet (which it may well do!).*

— *Leggings*

*Warm socks are a must.*

*Over a third of body heat is lost through your head. Cover it up!*

## ...AND ON TOP?

Outerwear can be expensive, depending on what material it is made from. Gore-tex material is highly waterproof and hard-wearing – but very costly. There are many cheaper alternatives – shop around to see what fits your needs and your price range.

Don't forget gloves, or mits, and a hat. A neck-warmer will also keep the cold out, especially when you take a tumble (*below*)!

### WET, WET, WET!

*Or rather dry, dry, dry! You will be a happier rider if you have waterproofed your outerwear (left), especially your boots and gloves, before you hit the slopes. Use Dubbin or a special waterproofing rub. You can also waterproof materials with a spray.*

*Pad yourself out with wrist guards and knee pads, or wear gloves with built-in wrist guards, and trousers with built-in knee pads.*

*Most riders wear soft boots which are more flexible than hard boots.*

11

# What to do first

Snowboarding can be quite strenuous, so it is a good idea to get in shape before you take to the slopes (*see page 30 for your warm-up*). If your body is not used to the demands of the activity, you are more likely to injure yourself by pulling a muscle (placing too much strain on a muscle). Increase your fitness by playing different sports, from in-line skating to football.

Now, it is time to get to a dry ski slope or some real snow – but it is important that you have a couple of lessons before setting off on your own.

**LESSONS**

*Take lessons with an instructor (above), qualified with the BSA (British Snowboarding Association) or the BASI (Britis Association of Snowboarding Instructors Ski schools abroad provide snowboardin lessons with English-speaking instructors*

## BINDINGS

If you have standard high-back bindings with two straps (*see page 8*), practise attaching and adjusting them. They can take a while to get used to! Be gentle with the clips, especially if it is cold because they will break if handled roughly. If they freeze up, take your board inside for ten minutes to defrost before using it.

Check that the straps are well out of the way before putting your feet in, or you might break a strap.

## BOARDING UP

The easiest and safest way to put on your board i to attach the safety leash on your board to your front leg when you are standing. This stops the board from sliding down the slope, without you! You can then sit down, facing down the hill; put your front foot into your binding and fasten it up (*below*). Then, put your back foot into the binding and fasten it up. Some experienced riders prefer to attach their bindings from a standing position (*left*)

**1**

**2**

**3**

## ET UP!

nce you have secured your leash and stened your bindings while sitting own, you are ready to get up. First, ractise this on the flat.

Turn yourself around so you are cing up the hill. To do this, vist the board into the air nd roll around its tail ⬜1 . ut your knees on the round. It is then easy push yourself up, sing your hands ⬚ . Be careful not to ver-balance.

As soon as you are standing, you must find the balanced or "ready" position. Keep your knees slightly bent and your stomach muscles tense. Turn your shoulders and head to face the same way as your feet ⬜3 . The ready position is one of the most important positions to learn – you will use it both as a beginner and as an experienced rider.

Apart from the angle of your head, the ready position stays the same, even if you are riding fakie, or backwards (*left*).

**POSITION CHECK**
*By keeping your
stomach muscles tight,
you will help to
maintain your balance.
Keep your knees
slightly bent.*

### ARE YOU READY?
Before riding, check that:
❊ **Your leash is attached**
❊ **Your boots and bindings are secure**
❊ **You are in the ready position**
❊ **Now, off you go!**

*lightly flex or tense your nkle joints.*

*his is your eel-side.*

*This is your toe-side.*

*This is your toe-edge.*

*This is your heel-edge.*

*Falling down...*

*...backwards (above)!*

*Go low to increase pressure (left).*

*Stand tall to reduce pressure (right).*

## FALLING FAST

When you feel yourself over-balancing backwards, bend your knees more, as if you are about to sit down (*left*). Only put your hands on the ground, protected by your wrist guards, when you have landed.

When you feel yourself over-balancing forwards, move as if you are about to kneel down; put your knees down to help you break your fall – at this point you will feel the benefit of your knee pads. Finish the fall onto your forearms (*right*).

*Going down... forwards!*

# Off you go!

Now that you are familiar with your equipment and the ready position, you can at last get moving, slowly! Make sure you have a good feel of the ready position (*see page 13*), and that you know how to fall over and get back up again (*see page 13*). Practise your pressure control technique (*left*) – this will not only help you to stop but it will also help you with more advanced moves (*see page 21*). Remember to wear your wrist guards and helmet, whether you are learning on snow or a dry ski slope.

## PRESSURE CONTROL

Practise changing the pressure of your weight on the base of your board (*above*). Stand tall to reduce the pressure; bend your knees and tense your legs to increase the pressure. Practise changing pressure from edge to edge. Stand still and rock from the toe-edge to the heel-edge on the flat. Try lifting your toes up when on a heel-edge and pointing them down when on a toe-edge.

### WANT A LIFT?
There are four main types of lift in a ski resort to get you up the mountain – chair-lifts, T-bars, button lifts and gondolas. Gondolas are easy because you take your board off. The others take a bit of getting used to.

To get on and off a T-bar, as shown in the sequence (*right*), take your back foot out of your bindings.

## SCOOTING ALONG

To get the feel of moving, practise scooting around on your board with your back foot out of your binding. Use your back foot to push, keeping your weight on your front foot (*left*). This must be done on the flat!

Once you are confident with this, with both boots in the bindings, use pressure control to slide down a gentle slope. Try it on your toe-edge and then your heel-edge. Try the "falling leaf" exercise – move your weight onto your front foot and then your back foot when sliding slowly down the hill.

*Even as you scoot, keep the ready position with your hands in front of you.*

Grab the bar with your front hand and place it between your legs. Put your back foot between your bindings and distribute your weight more onto your back foot for take-off. When you begin to move, stand up and even-out your weight. To get off, take the lift from between your legs; let go with your front hand and glide to a stop.

*STOP!*

*Stopping on your toe- or heel-edge is basically the same as a pressure control exercise. Practise by sliding down the hill on your toe- or heel-edge; then bend your knees to apply more pressure. This should bring you to a stop (above). Make sure you keep your weight slightly back, your hands forwards and your knees slightly bent.*

15

## SLALOM COURSE

A slalom run is a race course in which the gates are clos[e] together (*left*). As the racer goes towards the gate, he or she puts the board on an edge and presses hard, to mak[e] the board edge bite into the snow, creating a high speed carve (*s[ee] page 20*), close to the gate. A tight turn means a fast race. T[o] protect themselves from th[e] gates as they whiz arou[nd] them, racers wear protectiv[e] padding a[t] head and face gear.

### BOOTS AND BOARDS

*Racing snowboards, boots and bindings allow the riders to make high-speed carves. The boards are thin and long. The boots (left) are hard, similar to ski boots. They are used with "plate" bindings which clip onto the toe and heel of the boot. Racers use steep angles on their stance, usually between 45° and 60°.*

### DEBORAH ANTHONIAZ

**After only seven years racing, Deborah Anthoniaz became the Junior World Champion in giant slalom. Aged 19, she will now compete at senior level. Begin your racing by joining a club – they welcome all abilities.**

# Snowboard racing

In racing, speed is essential as riders are timed against the clock. They ride, between markers set in the snow, at incredible speeds – up to 80 km per hour. This racing is known as running gates. To race, you need to be very precise and have excellent edge control to increase your speed.

Riders often train in the summer and autumn, running gates on glaciers, huge areas of ice.

# Extreme riding

xtreme snowboarding, or free-riding off-piste in very ifficult conditions, is exciting and exhilarating – but it an be very dangerous. The rider should be very skilled nd experienced, and have the correct attitude, knowing is or her limits. An extreme rider always checks for valanche danger and wears a special transmitter called a leeper. High-pitched signals from this elp the rescue services to find riders ho are lost or buried in an avalanche.

## AVALANCHES

Avalanches are set off if layers of snow are disturbed, causing heavy slabs of snow to hurtle down the mountain. They are more likely to happen on steep slopes after a heavy snowfall. Many resorts use dynamite to clear such potentially dangerous areas of snow.

## CLIFF DROPS

or a successful cliff drop (*right*) the landing nust be steep, fairly smooth and soft. The un-out (the flat area at the bottom of the slope) must be long enough to prevent the rider hitting anything. The rider needs to have enough speed to clear any rocks.

## CHUTES

*As with cliffs, the extreme rider must check the entry and exit of the chute (a natural gulley, left), before attempting it. The steeper and narrower the chute, the faster the speed at the bottom and the longer the run-out needed.*

17

*UP YOU GO!*
*To climb a hill with your snowboard on, turn around so you are facing up the hill. Put both your hands on the ground in front of you and jump your feet up to meet them. This is quite hard work! Alternatively, release one foot from the bindings. Lift the board with your other foot and take a step, cutting the toe-edge into the snow (above).*

*If you have a long way to go, take your board off and walk!*

### THE FALL LINE

If you drop something at the top of a hill it will fall straight down the fall line – the direction in which gravity pulls you down the hill (*right*). If you stand tall on your board and take the pressure off the edges, the board will go down the fall line.

### TRAVERSING

The key to traversing (travelling across the hill, without losing too much height, *below*), is to turn your body the way you want to go. Keep in the ready position, with your hands in front of you. Flex your knee and ankle joints. Make sure that you are on an edge.

*If you turn to face too much up or down the hill you will "catch" an edge, and fall. This is when you are not clearly enough on an edge – the board becomes flat and the downhill edge digs into the snow – and over you go!*

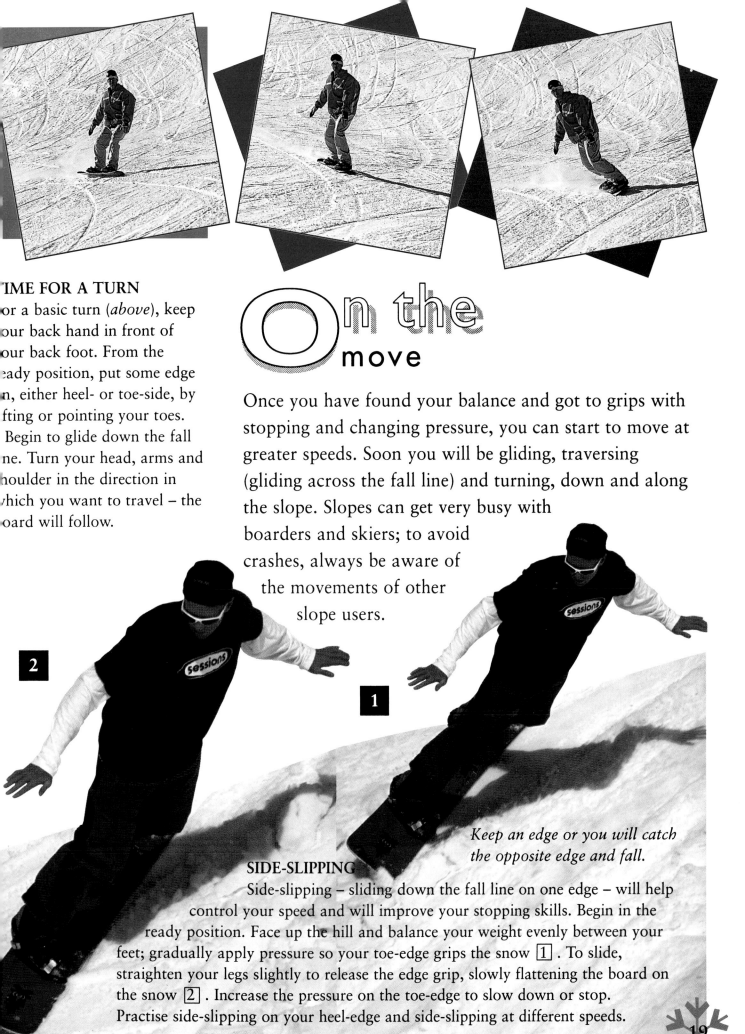

## TIME FOR A TURN

For a basic turn (*above*), keep your back hand in front of your back foot. From the ready position, put some edge on, either heel- or toe-side, by lifting or pointing your toes. Begin to glide down the fall line. Turn your head, arms and shoulder in the direction in which you want to travel – the board will follow.

# On the move

Once you have found your balance and got to grips with stopping and changing pressure, you can start to move at greater speeds. Soon you will be gliding, traversing (gliding across the fall line) and turning, down and along the slope. Slopes can get very busy with boarders and skiers; to avoid crashes, always be aware of the movements of other slope users.

**2**

**1**

*Keep an edge or you will catch the opposite edge and fall.*

### SIDE-SLIPPING

Side-slipping – sliding down the fall line on one edge – will help control your speed and will improve your stopping skills. Begin in the ready position. Face up the hill and balance your weight evenly between your feet; gradually apply pressure so your toe-edge grips the snow ☐1. To slide, straighten your legs slightly to release the edge grip, slowly flattening the board on the snow ☐2. Increase the pressure on the toe-edge to slow down or stop. Practise side-slipping on your heel-edge and side-slipping at different speeds.

19

# Twisting and turning

If you are confident with traversing, side-slipping and your basic turns, you are ready to try some toe-side and heel-side turns. Remember to begin from your ready position, with your hands in front of you. As you will be turning at greater speeds, it is advisable to wear your pads and a helmet to begin with. When you have conquered this turning technique you can try carving – an advanced turn in which the board does not slide but stays on its edge during the turn.

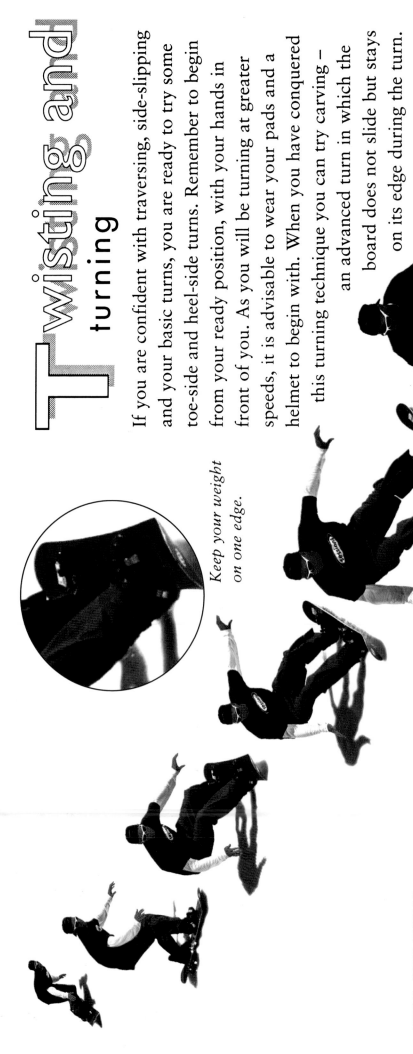

*Keep your weight on one edge.*

## HEEL-SIDE TURN

Get some speed up by side-slipping down the hill, toe-edge. Keeping most of your weight on your front foot, lower your heels to flatten the board. Lift up your toes to bring the board onto the heel-edge. Start the turn by leaning slightly backwards into the hill – don't sit down! Turn your upper body in the direction in which you want to turn and slide your back foot down the hill. As you feel the edge bite, press through your legs and follow the turn with your shoulders. As you complete the move, return to the side-slip position, heel-edge, ready for the toe-side turn.

## TOE-SIDE TURN

Build up some speed by side-slipping, heel-edge, down the hill. Transfer most of your weight over your front foot. Start the turn by slightly leaning into the hill with your shoulders. Flatten your board and you will feel it move down the fall line (*see page 18*). With your weight still mostly on your front foot, use your pressure skills (*see page 14*) to put your board onto the toe-edge. Don't twist your whole body, but turn your upper body to face towards the direction of the turn. Press through your legs and the board will follow the direction of your upper body.

*Your board is now on the toe-edge.*

*Move to the opposite edge as you turn.*

## MAKING THE LINK

To link turns, follow a heel-side turn immediately with a toe-side turn, as in the sequence pictured. Make sure that your shoulders follow the direction of your feet, from movement to movement. Move clearly from edge to edge – otherwise you will "catch" an edge and fall. When you turn, and especially when you link turns, you need to make sure that the way is clear. Always look where you are going!

## STRAIGHT AIRS

For your first air, find a small jump with a smooth, gentle landing. Practise going over the jump without taking air first. When you feel more confident, approach or hit the jump a little faster, and ollie (*see below*) as you get to the top. Make sure that your board is not on an edge when you take off or you will become unbalanced in the air.

Once you are used to being in the air, try some grabs – different ways of holding the board while you are in the air. As you take off, reach down with your back hand and grab in between your feet, toe-edge – this is an "indie".

*Style an air by "boning" it (left) – straightening one leg during a trick and holding the position while you are in the air.*

### OLLIEING

Before you learn to jump you need to learn to ollie. This is a basic trick which propels you into the air, without using a launch or hit. Ollieing is good fun and it's a great way to you keep your balance on the board.

*Before you ollie on a slope, practise on the flat.*

*Start in your ready position, with your hands in front of you. Begin moving in a straight line. Rock your weight onto your back foot* 1 *. Spring forwards and up off the tail of your board* 2 *.*

# Snowboarding trickery

Once you are confident and safe with the basic moves, you can try some tricks, from airs to ollies. Before you start any trick or variation, remember to use your ready position – without it you are more likely to lose control when you land. Tricks also look cooler and more stylish if the rider seems to be in control, without his or her arms and hands waving all over the place!

As you develop your ability to perform tricks, you can start to polish your own style. Take a look at other more experienced riders and try to copy their moves – but only attempt what you can do safely. Make up your own tricks and moves – with names too!

*FAKING IT OR SWITCHING IT? Riding fakie is riding backwards (tail first) or leading with the foot which usually follows. The technique for riding fakie is similar to that for riding forwards (nose first), except that you twist more with your hips. Make sure that you are looking in the direction in which you want to travel, checking that there are no people or obstacles in your way. Try to keep your weight centred, without leaning too far forwards. Practise riding fakie because it will help you later to learn some harder tricks. If you start a trick, such as an ollie (above), tail first, you are riding switch.*

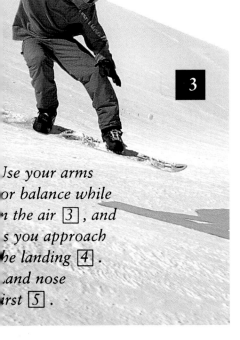

Use your arms for balance while in the air 3 , and as you approach the landing 4 , and nose first 5 .

# Advanced free-riding

Free-riding is about finding the places you like to ride and experimenting with tricks which you can perform safely. When you are confident with free-riding on the piste (a groomed slope where the snow is packed), you may want to try some off-piste riding.

The snow on an off-piste slope is powder (*see right*). Here you will find the most difficult runs on the mountain. Different types of snow mean that places will be better at different times during the season and the day. On-piste, or off-piste, always be aware of other slope users. Never ride fast in a beginners' area or if it is very busy.

### BUMPING AND SPEEDING

*Free-riding at high speeds (right) is also great fun, especially if the piste has just been groomed. Try some high speed carves. Feel your edges biting into the snow. Put more angle on your stance (see page 8) – this will make the edges hold even better.*

*Bumps and moguls are good fun if the snow is very mushy but are terrible if it is icy. A mogul is a large bump in the snow created when many people have turned in the same place. The easiest way to ride them is to turn in the gaps between each bump.*

# OFF-PISTE

Riding off-piste is one the greatest challenges, even for the most experienced snowboarder.

Only ever attempt to go off-piste when you are a competent and confident rider. Never go alone, and always tell an adult where you are going and at what time you expect to be back. Before going off-piste in the mountains check with the ski patrol if it is safe to do so. When you begin, look for snow which is approximately a boot's depth – any deeper and you may find it more hard-going than fun!

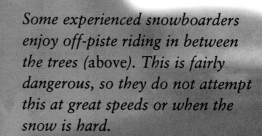

*Some experienced snowboarders enjoy off-piste riding in between the trees (above). This is fairly dangerous, so they do not attempt this at great speeds or when the snow is hard.*

### POWDER

*Powder snow is fresh, deep, light and dry – riding it is every boarder's dream. It is fairly easy to do as long as you remember to keep your weight on your back foot. It is also a good idea to set your bindings back from the centre of your board so you do not sink in the snow. There is nothing better than seeing a wide-open powder field with no tracks – and making the field your own (above).*

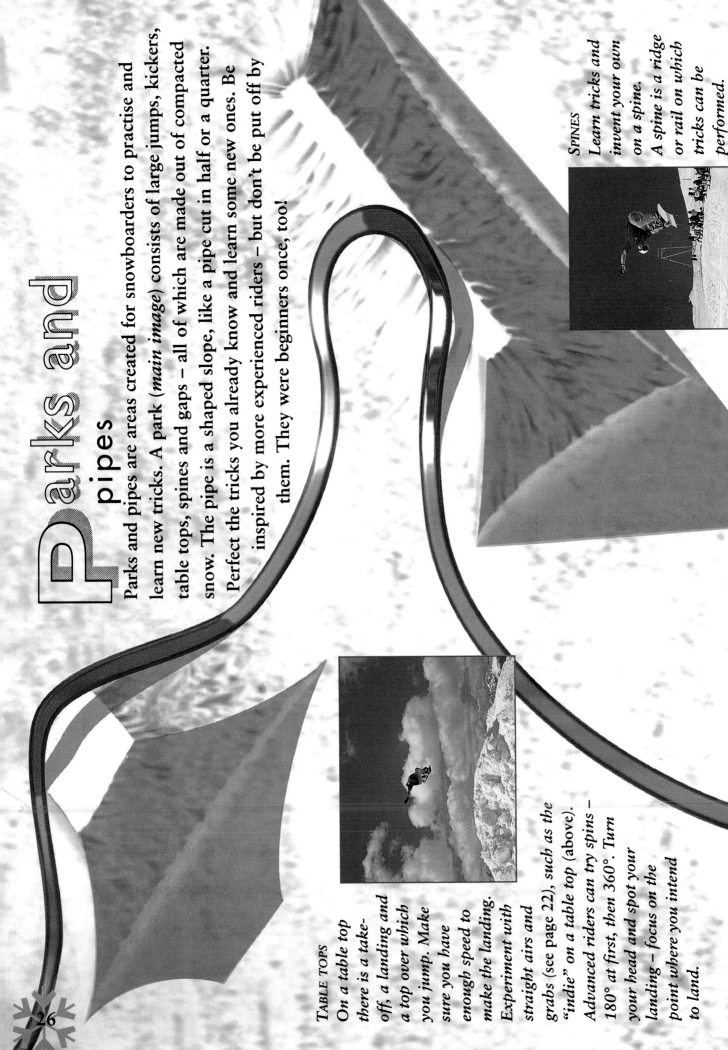

# Parks and pipes

Parks and pipes are areas created for snowboarders to practise and learn new tricks. A park (*main image*) consists of large jumps, kickers, table tops, spines and gaps – all of which are made out of compacted snow. The pipe is a shaped slope, like a pipe cut in half or a quarter. Perfect the tricks you already know and learn some new ones. Be inspired by more experienced riders – but don't be put off by them. They were beginners once, too!

*SPINES*
Learn tricks and invent your own on a spine.
A spine is a ridge or rail on which tricks can be performed.

*TABLE TOPS*
On a table top there is a take-off, a landing and a top over which you jump. Make sure you have enough speed to make the landing. Experiment with straight airs and grabs (see page 22), such as the "indie" on a table top (above).

Advanced riders can try spins – 180° at first, then 360°. Turn your head and spot your landing – focus on the point where you intend to land.

GAPS

These are like boxes except there is a gap instead of a flattened area (left). When you jump them you must make sure that you have enough speed or you will miss the landing and fall down the gap. Only jump a gap if you are sure you can clear it!

## IN THE PIPE

When you ride the pipe (above and right), don't worry about taking air from the walls – jumping from the sides. Begin by smoothly riding the transition (the curved area) to get used to the feel of the pipe. Ride to the top of the wall before turning round to jump back down again. Once you have got the hang of this, increase your speed so that you can get some air, then try a few grabs!

## STAY SAFE

Parks and pipes are fun, but unless you are fully protected and ride safely, you could injure yourself and others:

❄ Wear pads, guards and a helmet

❄ Be safe, and popular – always wait your turn before dropping into the pipe or park

❄ Unless you are landing, stay clear of landing areas

# Care of your snowboard

It is very important to take proper care of your kit, especially your board. Don't bang it on the ground to remove snow – brush it off.

When you are using your board, have it waxed at a workshop in a shop or resort at least once a week, to prevent the base from drying out.

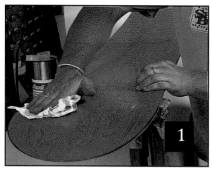

1 The base of the board is cleaned with some wax remover.

2 The edges are smoothed with a file. This file is quite sharp so care must be taken when using it.

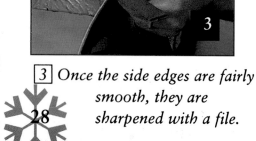

3 Once the side edges are fairly smooth, they are sharpened with a file.

*Using a file guide ensures that the edges are evenly filed.*

4 A metal brush or a scourer (above) is used to remove any filings left over.

5 Small holes can be filled with a substance called P-Tex. This is lit using a candle and dripped into the hole. P-Tex can burn your skin, so always be careful if you are in a workshop or near someone using P-Tex. The board is now ready for repair.

6 In the workshop, a special gun is used to melt the P-Tex into the hole in the snowboard.

7 The repairer checks to see if the P-Tex has filled in the hole.

8 Any excess P-Tex is removed by filing the base smooth with a fine file.

9 With the wax iron on a medium setting, wax is melted onto the board.

With regular waxing, your board will last longer and you will be able to ride faster.

[10] The wax is ironed into the board insuring even coverage. The iron is never left to rest on the base at any time.

[11] Any excess wax is scraped off with a plastic scraper when the wax is cool.

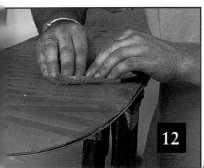

[12] The base of the board is then treated with a scratch pad to create small grooves in the wax on the board. As tiny drops of water move along the base of the board, it is easier for the board to go faster along the snow.

# Snowboard accessories

You will be able to find any accessories you might need in a good snowboard shop or via mail order through snowboard magazines. Special accessories, like avalanche bleepers, will have to be ordered from the manufacturer or bought at a good mountaineering shop.

## STREET GEAR

The sport of snowboarding is closely related to the fashion industry, and there are many inexpensive street-wear clothes to be found with snowboard influences. As snowboarding is a very close relative of skateboarding, many companies make both skate-and snowboard wear. This means snowboarders can look good both on and off the slope (*below*).

To find a good selection of the latest street-wear, visit your nearest skateboard or snowboard shop. Cool street wear means wearing clothes you feel comfortable in – don't be scared to be a bit different!

*IN YOUR POCKET*
Pocket-sized tools are ideal to take up the mountain, in case you need to tighten your bindings. Take a water bottle with you, too.

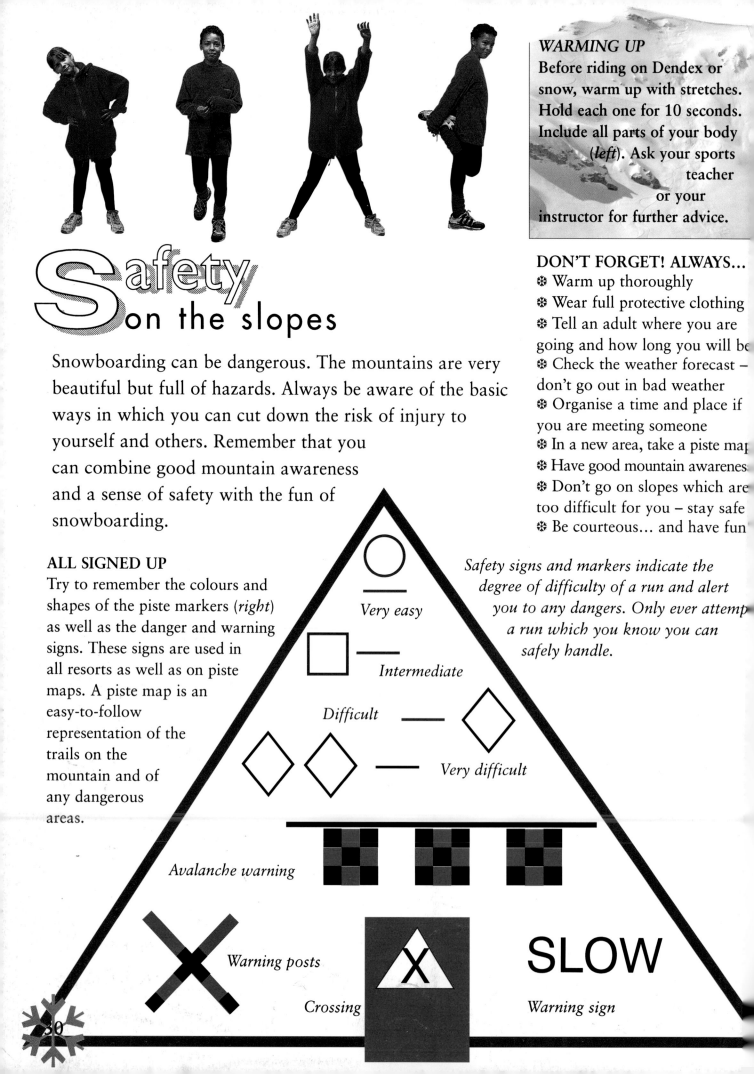

## WARMING UP

Before riding on Dendex or snow, warm up with stretches. Hold each one for 10 seconds. Include all parts of your body (*left*). Ask your sports teacher or your instructor for further advice.

# Safety on the slopes

Snowboarding can be dangerous. The mountains are very beautiful but full of hazards. Always be aware of the basic ways in which you can cut down the risk of injury to yourself and others. Remember that you can combine good mountain awareness and a sense of safety with the fun of snowboarding.

## DON'T FORGET! ALWAYS...

❄ Warm up thoroughly
❄ Wear full protective clothing
❄ Tell an adult where you are going and how long you will be
❄ Check the weather forecast – don't go out in bad weather
❄ Organise a time and place if you are meeting someone
❄ In a new area, take a piste map
❄ Have good mountain awareness
❄ Don't go on slopes which are too difficult for you – stay safe
❄ Be courteous... and have fun

## ALL SIGNED UP

Try to remember the colours and shapes of the piste markers (*right*) as well as the danger and warning signs. These signs are used in all resorts as well as on piste maps. A piste map is an easy-to-follow representation of the trails on the mountain and of any dangerous areas.

*Safety signs and markers indicate the degree of difficulty of a run and alert you to any dangers. Only ever attempt a run which you know you can safely handle.*

Very easy

Intermediate

Difficult

Very difficult

*Avalanche warning*

*Warning posts*

*Crossing*

SLOW

*Warning sign*

# Snowboard Speak

**Air** A jump.

**Binding** An attachment which secures the boot to the board.

**Bleeper** A transmitter which makes a bleeping noise.

**Bumps** Raised areas in the snow.

**Carve** A high-speed turn, in which the board stays on an edge.

**Dendex** The plastic material from which dry slopes are made.

**Edge** A side of the board which comes in contact with the snow.

**Extreme** An extreme sport involves skill and danger. Extreme snowboarding involves cliff jumps in the most challenging terrain.

**Fakie** Riding backwards or with the leading leg following.

**Flex** To contract or tighten.

**Free-riding** A snowboarding style which includes all styles.

**Free-style** A snowboarding style in which the rider takes air and rides the pipe.

**Gap** A table top with a gap in the middle over which you jump.

**Giant slalom** A long, timed race in which the markers are further apart than on a slalom.

**Goofy** Snowboarding with your right foot forwards.

**Grab** Arm and leg variations on a move.

**Half-pipe** A half-pipe shaped channel carved out in the snow.

**Heel-edge** The edge of the board on your heel-side.

**Heel-side** The side of your board behind your heels.

**Hit** Approaching a jump, or another word for a jump.

**Kicker** A steep jump.

**Ollieing** A launch into the air without using a jump.

**P-Tex** A material for mending holes in your board.

**Park** An area for boarders with jumps and tricks.

**Pipe** A half- or quarter-pipe shape, carved out in the snow.

**Pulling tricks** Doing stunts or special moves on a snowboard.

**Quarter-pipe** A quarter-pipe shaped channel carved out in the snow.

**Racing** Snowboarding against the clock.

**Regular** Snowboarding with your left foot forwards.

**Slalom** A timed race through a set of markers or gates.

**Spine** A ridge or rail on which you can perform tricks.

**Stance angle** The angle at which you set your bindings.

**Stance width** The distance between your bindings.

**Switch** Performing a trick, such as an ollie, backwards.

**Table top** A raised area of snow over which riders can jump and perform tricks.

**Terrain** The type of land over which you ride.

**Toe-edge** The edge of the board on your toe-side.

**Toe-side** The side of your board in front of your toes.

# Index

Photo Credits: *Abbreviations: t-top, m-middle, b-bottom, r-right, l-left*

All the pictures in this book were supplied by Snowboarding UK magazine except for the following: pages 1, 4-5, 7 all, 17t, 24b, 24-25 & 25 – Frank Spooner Pictures; 2, 3, 8tm, 10, 11l, 12t & b, 14t, 18tl, 28-29 all & 30 – Roger Vlitos.

The publishers would like to thank the Tamworth Snowdome, Boardwise in Chiswick, Boardwise in Tamworth and Snowboarding UK for their help and co-operation in the preparation of this book.